31 Days of Declarations

A Journey of Faith, Hope and

Victory

Dr. Tyrone T. Lewis, Sr.

Introduction

Welcome to *31 Days of Declarations: A Journey of Faith, Hope, and Victory.* This book is designed to guide you into a deeper understanding of God's Word, helping you align your thoughts, words, and heart with His truth. Each day provides a powerful opportunity to declare God's promises over your life, strengthen your faith, and walk boldly in the purpose He has designed for you.

Our words carry incredible power. Proverbs 18:21 reminds us, *"The tongue has the power of life and death, and those who love it will eat its fruit."* What we speak over ourselves and others can shape our lives, influence our circumstances, and reflect the faith we have in God. Through this book, you will learn to speak life by declaring God's truth into every area of your life—your identity, relationships, health, finances, and spiritual growth.

Each day includes:

- An inspirational quote to refocus your heart and mind on God's promises

- Relevant scriptures to anchor your declarations in the Word of God

- Declarations of faith to speak over your life with confidence and authority

- A prayer to invite God's presence and power into your day

This 31-day journey is not just a ritual or routine; it is an invitation to partner with God through the power of His Word. As you declare His promises, you are choosing to align your heart with His will and invite His blessings into your life. You will experience greater peace, joy, and strength as you declare His truth and watch it transform your perspective.

Whether you are in a season of waiting, healing, growth, or victory, this book is for you. It is for anyone who desires to renew their mind, grow in faith, and live boldly as a child of God. Each chapter serves as a stepping stone to help you overcome discouragement, embrace your identity in Christ, and walk confidently in His promises.

How to Use This Book

1. Read one chapter each day for 31 days, or as often as you need encouragement.

2. Speak the declarations out loud with faith and confidence.

3. Meditate on the scriptures and personalize them in your prayers.

Remember, the Word of God is alive and active (Hebrews 4:12). When you declare it boldly, God's power is released into your life. Over the next 31 days, expect transformation, breakthrough, and a renewed awareness of God's presence in every area of your life.

Let's begin this life-changing journey together. The best is yet to come!

In His Grace,
Dr. Tyrone Lewis, Sr.

Acknowledgments

First and foremost, I want to thank my incredible wife, Chiquita Lewis, for always believing in me, encouraging me, and pushing me to step into the fullness of God's purpose for my life. Your unwavering support, love, and faith have been the fuel behind this journey. Thank you for standing by my side and reminding me daily of the power of God's promises.

To my church family at Triumph Church of Gulfport, I am forever grateful for your prayers, love, and encouragement. You have been a source of strength and inspiration, and I am honored to walk this journey of faith with you. Thank you for being a community that embodies hope, unity, and unwavering trust in God.

To my spiritual father, Apostle Travis Jennings, thank you for your mentorship, guidance, and for pouring into me with wisdom and truth. Your leadership and example have challenged me to grow spiritually and step boldly into my calling. I am deeply grateful for the seeds of faith and courage you have planted in my life.

Finally, I give all glory and honor to God, who is the author of this book and the author of my life. Without Him, none of this would be possible.

Thank you all for being a part of this journey. Your love, faith, and encouragement have made this book a reality.

With Gratitude,

Dr. Tyrone Lewis, Sr.

Day 1: Identity in Christ

Inspirational Quote

"When you know who you are in Christ, you stop searching for validation from the world."

Scriptures

- "Therefore, if anyone is in Christ, the new creation has come: The old has gone, the new is here!" (2 Corinthians 5:17)

- "But you are a chosen people, a royal priesthood, a holy nation, God's special possession." (1 Peter 2:9)

Declarations

1. I declare that I am a new creation in Christ.

2. I am chosen, loved, and set apart by God.

3. I declare that my past does not define me—Christ does.

4. I am redeemed and made righteous through Jesus.

5. I am a child of God and an heir to His promises.

6. I declare that I walk confidently in my God-given identity.

7. My life reflects the light and love of Christ.

Encouraging Affirmations

Speak these truths over yourself daily and anchor your heart in your true identity:

- I am a new creation in Christ (2 Corinthians 5:17).

- I am chosen and appointed by God (1 Peter 2:9).

- I am fearfully and wonderfully made (Psalm 139:14).

- I am God's workmanship, created for good works (Ephesians 2:10).

- I am forgiven and redeemed (Colossians 1:13–14).

- I am loved with an everlasting love (Jeremiah 31:3).

- I belong to God (Romans 8:16).

Prayer

Father God, thank You for giving me a new identity in Christ. Help me to see myself the way You see me—chosen, loved, and redeemed. Remove any lies that try to define me by my past or my failures. Teach me to walk boldly and confidently as Your child. In Jesus' name, Amen.

Day 2: Walking in God's Purpose

Inspirational Quote

"You were not created by accident—God designed you with intention and purpose."

Scriptures

- "For we are God's workmanship, created in Christ Jesus to do good works, which God prepared in advance for us to do." (Ephesians 2:10)

- "Many are the plans in a person's heart, but it is the Lord's purpose that prevails." (Proverbs 19:21)

Declarations

1. I declare that I was created with divine purpose.

2. God has prepared good works for me to accomplish.

3. I declare that I walk confidently in the path God has set before me.

4. My steps are ordered by the Lord.

5. I trust God's timing and direction for my life.

8

6. I declare that nothing can stop God's purpose for me.

7. I live intentionally, aligned with God's will.

Encouraging Affirmations

Speak these truths over yourself daily and embrace your God-given purpose:

- I am God's workmanship, created for good works (Ephesians 2:10).

- The Lord directs my steps (Proverbs 16:9).

- God works all things together for my good (Romans 8:28).

- I am called according to His purpose (Romans 8:28).

- The Lord fulfills His purpose for me (Psalm 138:8).

- I trust in the Lord with all my heart (Proverbs 3:5–6).

- God's plans for me are for hope and a future (Jeremiah 29:11).

Prayer

Father God, thank You for creating me with intention and purpose. Help me to trust Your direction and follow the path You have prepared for me. Give me clarity, courage, and obedience as I walk in Your will. Let my life bring glory to You. In Jesus' name, Amen.

Day 3: Overcoming Fear

Inspirational Quote

"Fear may knock at your door, but faith answers with confidence in God."

Scriptures

- "For God has not given us a spirit of fear, but of power, love, and a sound mind." (2 Timothy 1:7)

- "When I am afraid, I put my trust in You." (Psalm 56:3)

Declarations

1. I declare that fear has no authority over my life.

2. God has given me power, love, and a sound mind.

3. I declare that I walk by faith and not by fear.

4. I trust God completely in every situation.

5. I declare that God's perfect love casts out all fear.

6. I am courageous because the Lord is with me.

7. I choose faith over anxiety and peace over worry.

Encouraging Affirmations

Speak these truths over yourself daily and stand firm in courage:

- God has not given me a spirit of fear (2 Timothy 1:7).

- When I am afraid, I trust in the Lord (Psalm 56:3).

- The Lord is with me; I will not be afraid (Isaiah 41:10).

- Perfect love drives out fear (1 John 4:18).

- The Lord is my light and my salvation—whom shall I fear? (Psalm 27:1).

- I am strong and courageous because God goes with me (Deuteronomy 31:6).

- The peace of God guards my heart and mind (Philippians 4:7).

Prayer

Father God, I surrender every fear and anxiety to You. Fill my heart with Your peace and courage. Help me to trust You fully, even when circumstances feel uncertain.

Strengthen my faith and remind me daily that You are always with me. In Jesus' name, Amen.

Day 4: Living in God's Peace

Inspirational Quote

"God's peace is not the absence of trouble—it is His presence in the middle of it."

Scriptures

- "Peace I leave with you; My peace I give you. I do not give to you as the world gives. Do not let your hearts be troubled and do not be afraid." (John 14:27)

- "And the peace of God, which transcends all understanding, will guard your hearts and your minds in Christ Jesus." (Philippians 4:7)

Declarations

1. I declare that God's peace fills my heart and mind.

2. I refuse to let anxiety control my thoughts.

3. I declare that I trust God completely in every situation.

4. His peace guards me day and night.

5. I choose calmness over chaos and faith over fear.

6. I declare that my home and life are covered in God's peace.

7. I rest confidently in the presence of the Lord.

Encouraging Affirmations

Speak these truths over yourself daily and remain anchored in peace:

- Jesus gives me His peace (John 14:27).

- The peace of God guards my heart and mind (Philippians 4:7).

- I cast all my anxiety on Him because He cares for me (1 Peter 5:7).

- The Lord blesses me with peace (Numbers 6:26).

- I will lie down and sleep in peace, for the Lord keeps me safe (Psalm 4:8).

- I keep my mind stayed on Him, and He keeps me in perfect peace (Isaiah 26:3).

- The Lord is my shepherd; I lack nothing (Psalm 23:1).

Prayer

Father God, thank You for the gift of Your peace. In moments of stress and uncertainty, remind me that You are in control. Guard my heart and mind from anxiety and fill me with calm assurance. Help me to trust You fully and rest in Your presence. In Jesus' name, Amen.

Day 5: Strength in Weakness

Inspirational Quote

"Your weakness is not a limitation—it is an invitation for God's power to be revealed."

Scriptures

- "But He said to me, 'My grace is sufficient for you, for My power is made perfect in weakness.'" (2 Corinthians 12:9)

- "I can do all things through Christ who strengthens me." (Philippians 4:13)

Declarations

1. I declare that God's grace is sufficient for me.

2. His strength is perfected in my weakness.

3. I declare that I am strong through Christ who strengthens me.

4. I will not be discouraged by my limitations.

5. God's power works mightily within me.

6. I declare that every challenge becomes an opportunity for God's glory.

7. I rely on God's strength rather than my own.

Encouraging Affirmations

Speak these truths over yourself daily and draw strength from the Lord:

- God's grace is sufficient for me (2 Corinthians 12:9).

- When I am weak, then I am strong (2 Corinthians 12:10).

- I can do all things through Christ who strengthens me (Philippians 4:13).

- The Lord is the strength of my life (Psalm 27:1).

- Those who hope in the Lord renew their strength (Isaiah 40:31).

- The joy of the Lord is my strength (Nehemiah 8:10).

- God is my refuge and strength, an ever-present help in trouble (Psalm 46:1).

Prayer (From Day 5: Strength in Weakness)

Father God, I thank You that I do not have to rely on my own strength. In moments when I feel weak, remind me that Your grace is enough. Fill me with Your power and courage to face every challenge. Let Your strength be evident in my life. In Jesus' name, Amen.

Day 6: God's Provision
Inspirational Quote

"Where God guides, He provides."

Scriptures

- "And my God will meet all your needs according to the riches of His glory in Christ Jesus." (Philippians 4:19)

- "The Lord is my shepherd; I lack nothing." (Psalm 23:1)

Declarations

1. I declare that God is my provider.

2. All my needs are supplied according to His riches in glory.

3. I declare that I lack nothing because the Lord is my shepherd.

4. God provides for me spiritually, physically, and financially.

5. I trust God to open the right doors at the right time.

6. I declare that blessings and favor surround my life.

7. I live with confidence, knowing God cares for me.

Encouraging Affirmations

Speak these truths over yourself daily and trust in God's faithful provision:

- My God supplies all my needs (Philippians 4:19).
- The Lord is my shepherd; I shall not want (Psalm 23:1).
- I seek first the kingdom of God, and all these things are added to me (Matthew 6:33).
- God is able to bless me abundantly (2 Corinthians 9:8).
- The Lord provides for those who fear Him (Psalm 34:9–10).

- Every good and perfect gift comes from God
  (James 1:17).
- The Lord will provide (Genesis 22:14).

Prayer

Father God, thank You for being my provider. I trust You to meet every need in my life according to Your perfect will. Help me to rely fully on You and not worry about tomorrow. Increase my faith as I depend on Your faithful provision. In Jesus' name, Amen.

Day 7: Faith That Moves Mountains

Inspirational Quote

"Faith does not deny the mountain—it speaks to it and believes it will move."

Scriptures

- "Truly I tell you, if you have faith as small as a mustard seed… nothing will be impossible for you." (Matthew 17:20)
- "Have faith in God… whoever says to this mountain, 'Be taken up and thrown into the sea,'

and does not doubt in his heart… it will be done for him." (Mark 11:22–23)

Declarations

1. I declare that my faith is strong and unwavering.
2. Even small faith produces great results.
3. I declare that the mountains in my life are moving.
4. I believe God for the impossible.
5. Doubt has no place in my heart.
6. I declare that nothing is impossible with God.
7. I walk by faith and not by sight.

Encouraging Affirmations

Speak these truths over yourself daily and strengthen your faith:

- I have faith as small as a mustard seed (Matthew 17:20).
- Nothing is impossible with God (Luke 1:37).
- I walk by faith, not by sight (2 Corinthians 5:7).
- Without faith it is impossible to please God (Hebrews 11:6).
- If I believe, I will receive what I ask in prayer (Matthew 21:22).
- The righteous live by faith (Romans 1:17).

- Faith is confidence in what I hope for (Hebrews 11:1).

Prayer

Father God, increase my faith. Help me to trust You beyond what I see and feel. Teach me to speak to the mountains in my life with confidence in Your power. Remove doubt and strengthen my belief in Your promises. I declare that through You, nothing is impossible. In Jesus' name, Amen.

Day 8: Healing and Wholeness

Inspirational Quote

"God's healing restores not only the body, but the heart, mind, and soul."

Scriptures

- "He heals the brokenhearted and binds up their wounds." (Psalm 147:3)
- "But He was pierced for our transgressions… and by His wounds we are healed." (Isaiah 53:5)

Declarations

1. I declare that God is restoring my body, mind, and spirit.
2. I receive God's healing and wholeness today.
3. I declare that every broken place in my life is being made whole.
4. The healing power of Jesus flows through me.
5. I am strengthened and renewed daily.
6. I declare that sickness and pain do not have the final word.
7. God's peace and health fill my life.

Encouraging Affirmations

Speak these truths over yourself daily and stand firm in faith for healing:

- The Lord heals the brokenhearted (Psalm 147:3).
- By His wounds I am healed (Isaiah 53:5).
- The Lord sustains me and restores me (Psalm 41:3).
- I will live and declare the works of the Lord (Psalm 118:17).
- Jesus went about doing good and healing all (Acts 10:38).
- The prayer of faith brings healing (James 5:15).
- The Lord blesses me with peace and wholeness (Numbers 6:26).

Prayer

Father God, I thank You for being my healer. I ask for Your restoring power to touch every area of my life—physically, emotionally, and spiritually. Heal what is broken, renew what is weary, and make me whole again. I trust in Your compassion and power. In Jesus' name, Amen.

Day 9: Walking in Obedience

Inspirational Quote

"Obedience is not about perfection—it is about trusting God enough to follow His voice."

Scriptures

- "If you love Me, keep My commands." (John 14:15)
- "Trust in the Lord with all your heart and lean not on your own understanding; in all your ways submit to Him, and He will make your paths straight." (Proverbs 3:5–6)

Declarations

1. I declare that I walk in obedience to God's Word.
2. I choose God's will over my own desires.

3. I declare that obedience brings blessing and direction.

4. I trust God even when I do not fully understand.

5. My heart is sensitive to the voice of the Holy Spirit.

6. I declare that my steps are ordered by the Lord.

7. I live a life that honors and pleases God.

Encouraging Affirmations

Speak these truths over yourself daily and commit to faithful obedience:

- If I love God, I keep His commands (John 14:15).

- The Lord directs my steps when I trust Him (Proverbs 3:5–6).

- Blessed are those who hear the Word of God and obey it (Luke 11:28).

- I am not just a hearer of the Word, but a doer (James 1:22).

- Obedience is better than sacrifice (1 Samuel 15:22).

- The Lord rewards those who diligently seek Him (Hebrews 11:6).

- I delight in doing God's will (Psalm 40:8).

Prayer

Father God, help me to walk in obedience each day. Give me the courage to follow Your direction, even when it is difficult. Soften my heart to hear Your voice and strengthen my faith to act on it. May my life reflect my love for You through faithful obedience. In Jesus' name, Amen.

Day 10: God's Favor

Inspirational Quote

"God's favor opens doors no one can shut and makes a way where there seems to be none."

Scriptures

- "Surely, Lord, You bless the righteous; You surround them with Your favor as with a shield." (Psalm 5:12)
- "For You, O Lord, will bless the righteous; with favor You will surround him as with a shield." (Psalm 5:12 NKJV)

Declarations

1. I declare that God's favor surrounds my life like a shield.
2. Doors of opportunity open for me according to God's will.
3. I declare that I walk in divine favor and blessing.
4. God's grace sets me apart and brings increase.

5. I receive favor with God and with people.

6. I declare that what I do prospers under God's hand.

7. The Lord's goodness and favor follow me daily.

Encouraging Affirmations

Speak these truths over yourself daily and walk confidently in God's favor:

- I am surrounded with God's favor as with a shield (Psalm 5:12).
- The Lord makes His face shine upon me (Numbers 6:24–26).
- I have favor with God and with people (Luke 2:52).
- God goes before me and prepares the way (Deuteronomy 31:8).
- The Lord grants me success according to His will (Proverbs 16:3).
- Surely goodness and mercy follow me all the days of my life (Psalm 23:6).
- The Lord establishes the work of my hands (Psalm 90:17).

Prayer

Father God, thank You for Your divine favor over my life. Open doors that align with Your purpose for me and close those that are not from You. Surround me with Your grace and let Your goodness be evident in everything I do. May Your favor bring glory to Your name. In Jesus' name, Amen.

Day 11: Walking in Faith

Inspirational Quote

"Faith is not seeing the whole path—it is trusting God with the next step."

Scriptures

- "For we live by faith, not by sight." (2 Corinthians 5:7)
- "Now faith is confidence in what we hope for and assurance about what we do not see." (Hebrews 11:1)

Declarations

1. I declare that I walk by faith and not by sight.
2. I trust God even when I cannot see the outcome.
3. I declare that my confidence is rooted in God's promises.
4. I step forward boldly, knowing God is with me.
5. Doubt does not control my decisions—faith does.

6. I declare that my faith grows stronger each day.

7. I rely on God's Word as my foundation and guide.

Encouraging Affirmations

Speak these truths over yourself daily and strengthen your walk of faith:

- I live by faith, not by sight (2 Corinthians 5:7).
- Faith gives me confidence in what I hope for (Hebrews 11:1).
- Without faith it is impossible to please God (Hebrews 11:6).
- The righteous will live by faith (Romans 1:17).
- I trust in the Lord with all my heart (Proverbs 3:5).
- God is faithful to fulfill His promises (Numbers 23:19).
- I will see the goodness of the Lord (Psalm 27:13).

Prayer

Father God, help me to walk by faith in every area of my life. Strengthen my trust in You when circumstances seem uncertain. Teach me to rely on Your promises and not my own understanding. Lead me step by step as I follow You in faith. In Jesus' name, Amen.

Day 12: Victory Over Temptation

Inspirational Quote

"Temptation may come, but through Christ, victory is always possible."

Scriptures

- "No temptation has overtaken you except what is common to mankind. And God is faithful; He will not let you be tempted beyond what you can bear... He will also provide a way out so that you can endure it." (1 Corinthians 10:13)
- "Submit yourselves, then, to God. Resist the devil, and he will flee from you." (James 4:7)

Declarations

1. I declare that I have victory over every temptation.
2. God always provides a way of escape for me.
3. I declare that I am strengthened by the Holy Spirit to stand firm.
4. I resist the enemy and remain steadfast in faith.
5. I choose obedience over compromise.
6. I declare that my mind and heart are aligned with God's truth.
7. I walk in self-control and spiritual strength.

Encouraging Affirmations (Day 12: Victory Over Temptation)

Speak these truths over yourself daily and stand firm against temptation:

- God provides a way out of every temptation (1 Corinthians 10:13).
- I resist the devil, and he flees from me (James 4:7).
- I put on the full armor of God (Ephesians 6:11).
- I take every thought captive to obey Christ (2 Corinthians 10:5).
- Blessed is the one who perseveres under trial (James 1:12).
- The Lord strengthens me in times of testing (Psalm 18:32).
- I am more than a conqueror through Christ (Romans 8:37).

Prayer

Father God, thank You for giving me the strength to overcome temptation. Help me to recognize the way of escape You provide and to choose obedience each time. Guard my heart and mind, and empower me to stand firm in faith. I declare victory through Jesus Christ. In His name, Amen.

Day 13: God's Guidance and Wisdom

Inspirational Quote

"When you seek God's wisdom, He directs your steps with clarity and purpose."

Scriptures

- "If any of you lacks wisdom, you should ask God, who gives generously to all without finding fault, and it will be given to you." (James 1:5)
- "Your word is a lamp to my feet and a light to my path." (Psalm 119:105)

Declarations

1. I declare that God gives me wisdom generously.
2. I seek God's direction in every decision I make.
3. I declare that His Word lights my path.
4. I trust God to guide my steps daily.
5. I walk in discernment and understanding.
6. I declare that confusion has no place in my life.
7. The Holy Spirit leads me into truth and clarity.

Encouraging Affirmations

Speak these truths over yourself daily and walk confidently in God's guidance:

- God gives me wisdom when I ask (James 1:5).
- The Lord directs my steps (Proverbs 16:9).
- His Word is a lamp to my feet (Psalm 119:105).
- I trust in the Lord, and He makes my paths straight (Proverbs 3:5–6).
- The Holy Spirit guides me into all truth (John 16:13).
- The Lord gives wisdom; from His mouth come knowledge and understanding (Proverbs 2:6).
- I have the mind of Christ (1 Corinthians 2:16).

Prayer

Father God, I ask for Your wisdom and guidance today. Direct my thoughts, decisions, and actions according to Your will. Remove confusion and replace it with clarity. Help me to trust Your leading and walk confidently in Your truth. In Jesus' name, Amen.

Day 14: Joy in Every Season

Inspirational Quote

"Joy is not determined by your season—it is rooted in your Savior."

Scriptures

- "Rejoice in the Lord always. I will say it again: Rejoice!" (Philippians 4:4)
- "Weeping may stay for the night, but rejoicing comes in the morning." (Psalm 30:5)

Declarations

1. I declare that my joy is rooted in the Lord.
2. I choose joy regardless of my circumstances.
3. I declare that sorrow does not have the final word.
4. The joy of the Lord is my strength.
5. I trust that every season has purpose.
6. I declare that God renews my hope daily.
7. My heart overflows with joy because God is faithful.

Encouraging Affirmations

Speak these truths over yourself daily and embrace joy in every season:

- I rejoice in the Lord always (Philippians 4:4).
- Weeping may endure for a night, but joy comes in the morning (Psalm 30:5).
- The joy of the Lord is my strength (Nehemiah 8:10).
- God fills me with joy and peace as I trust in Him (Romans 15:13).
- I consider it joy when I face trials (James 1:2).

- My heart is glad because I trust in the Lord (Psalm 28:7).
- In His presence there is fullness of joy (Psalm 16:11).

Prayer

Father God, thank You for the gift of joy that comes from knowing You. Help me to remain joyful in every season, whether in celebration or challenge. Strengthen my heart when I feel weary and remind me that true joy comes from Your presence. Fill my life with lasting joy that reflects Your goodness. In Jesus' name, Amen.

Day 15: Declaring God's Promises

Inspirational Quote

"When you declare God's promises, you align your words with His power."

Scriptures

- "For no matter how many promises God has made, they are 'Yes' in Christ." (2 Corinthians 1:20)
- "Heaven and earth will pass away, but My words will never pass away." (Matthew 24:35)

Declarations

1. I declare that God's promises are true and faithful.

2. Every promise spoken over my life is "Yes" and "Amen" in Christ.

3. I declare that God's Word stands firm forever.

4. I speak life and truth over my circumstances.

5. I stand confidently on the promises of God.

6. I declare that what God has spoken will come to pass.

7. My faith grows stronger as I proclaim His Word.

Encouraging Affirmations

Speak these truths over yourself daily and boldly declare God's promises:

- God's promises are "Yes" in Christ (2 Corinthians 1:20).

- His Word will never pass away (Matthew 24:35).

- The Lord is faithful to all His promises (Psalm 145:13).

- God is not a man, that He should lie (Numbers 23:19).

- His promises give me hope (Hebrews 10:23).

- I hide God's Word in my heart (Psalm 119:11).

- The Word of God is living and active (Hebrews 4:12).

Prayer

Father God, thank You for the promises found in Your Word. Help me to stand firm on Your truth and declare it boldly over my life. Strengthen my faith as I trust in what You have spoken. May Your promises guide my thoughts, shape my words, and anchor my heart. In Jesus' name, Amen.

Day 16: Boldness in Faith

Inspirational Quote

"Bold faith does not shrink back—it steps forward, trusting God completely."

Scriptures

- "Let us then approach God's throne of grace with confidence, so that we may receive mercy and find grace to help us in our time of need." (Hebrews 4:16)
- "The wicked flee though no one pursues, but the righteous are as bold as a lion." (Proverbs 28:1)

Declarations

1. I declare that I approach God with confidence and boldness.
2. I am courageous because my faith is rooted in Christ.
3. I declare that fear will not silence my faith.
4. I stand firm in God's promises without hesitation.
5. I speak truth with love and confidence.
6. I declare that the Holy Spirit empowers me to be bold.
7. I step forward in faith, trusting God with the outcome.

Encouraging Affirmations

Speak these truths over yourself daily and walk in fearless faith:

- I approach God's throne with confidence (Hebrews 4:16).
- I am bold as a lion because I am righteous in Christ (Proverbs 28:1).
- God has not given me a spirit of fear (2 Timothy 1:7).
- The Lord is my helper; I will not be afraid (Hebrews 13:6).

- I can do all things through Christ who strengthens me (Philippians 4:13).
- The Spirit gives me power and courage (Acts 1:8).
- I will not shrink back, but believe (Hebrews 10:39).

Prayer

Father God, fill me with boldness in my faith. Help me to trust You without hesitation and to stand confidently on Your Word. Remove fear and doubt, and replace them with courage and strength. Empower me through Your Spirit to live boldly for You each day. In Jesus' name, Amen.

Day 17: Protection and Safety

Inspirational Quote

"God's protection is not fragile—it is faithful, constant, and unshakable."

Scriptures

- "The Lord is my refuge and my fortress, my God, in whom I trust." (Psalm 91:2)
- "The Lord will keep you from all harm—He will watch over your life." (Psalm 121:7)

Declarations

1. I declare that the Lord is my refuge and my fortress.

2. I am covered and protected by Almighty God.

3. I declare that no weapon formed against me shall prosper.

4. The Lord watches over me and keeps me safe day and night.

5. I declare that God's angels guard me in all my ways.

6. Fear has no place in my life because God is my defender.

7. I rest confidently in God's divine protection and peace.

Encouraging Affirmations

Speak these truths over yourself daily and walk in confidence and security:

- The Lord is my refuge and fortress; I trust in Him (Psalm 91:2).

- No weapon formed against me shall prosper (Isaiah 54:17).

- The Lord watches over my coming and going both now and forevermore (Psalm 121:8).

- God commands His angels concerning me to guard me in all my ways (Psalm 91:11).

- The name of the Lord is a strong tower; I run to Him and am safe (Proverbs 18:10).

- The Lord is my light and my salvation—whom shall
  I fear? (Psalm 27:1).

- God is my shield and my defender (Psalm 3:3).

Prayer

Father God, thank You for being my refuge and my
protector. I place my trust fully in You. Cover me
and my loved ones with Your divine protection.
Guard our steps, our homes, and our lives.
Remove fear from our hearts and replace it with
confidence in Your faithful care. In Jesus' name,
Amen.

Day 18: God's Faithfulness

Inspirational Quote

"God's faithfulness is not based on our
circumstances—it is rooted in His unchanging
character."

Scriptures

- "Because of the Lord's great love we are not
  consumed, for His compassions never fail. They
  are new every morning; great is Your faithfulness."
  (Lamentations 3:22–23)

- "He who calls you is faithful, and He will do it." (1 Thessalonians 5:24)

Declarations

1. I declare that God is faithful in every season of my life.
2. His mercies toward me are new every morning.
3. I declare that God fulfills every promise He has spoken.
4. Even when I am uncertain, God remains constant and true.
5. I trust in God's faithfulness over my past, present, and future.
6. God's love for me never fails.
7. I stand secure because the One who called me is faithful.

Encouraging Affirmations

Speak these truths over yourself daily and rest in God's unchanging faithfulness:

- Great is God's faithfulness toward me (Lamentations 3:23).
- The Lord is faithful in all His words and kind in all His works (Psalm 145:13).

- Not one of God's good promises has ever failed (Joshua 21:45).
- God is not a man that He should lie; what He promises, He fulfills (Numbers 23:19).
- The Lord will never leave me nor forsake me (Deuteronomy 31:6).
- The One who calls me is faithful, and He will do it (1 Thessalonians 5:24).
- Jesus Christ is the same yesterday, today, and forever (Hebrews 13:8).

Prayer

Father God, thank You for Your unwavering faithfulness in my life. Even when I cannot see the full picture, I trust that You are working all things for my good. Remind me daily that Your promises are sure and Your love never fails. Help me to stand firm in faith, knowing You are always faithful. In Jesus' name, Amen.

Day 19: Freedom in Christ

Inspirational Quote

"True freedom is not found in escaping life's struggles, but in living fully in Christ's victory."

Scriptures

- "It is for freedom that Christ has set us free. Stand firm, then, and do not let yourselves be burdened again by a yoke of slavery." (Galatians 5:1)
- "So if the Son sets you free, you will be free indeed." (John 8:36)

Declarations

1. I declare that I am free because Christ has set me free.
2. I am no longer bound by fear, guilt, or shame.
3. I declare that I walk in the liberty and victory found in Jesus.
4. I am released from the power of sin and made alive in Christ.
5. I declare that there is no condemnation over my life.
6. I stand firm in the freedom God has given me.
7. I live confidently as a child of God, redeemed and restored.

Encouraging Affirmations

Speak these truths over yourself daily and walk boldly in your freedom:

- It is for freedom that Christ has set me free (Galatians 5:1).

- If the Son sets me free, I am free indeed (John 8:36).
- There is now no condemnation for those who are in Christ Jesus (Romans 8:1).
- I have been delivered from darkness and brought into God's kingdom (Colossians 1:13).
- Where the Spirit of the Lord is, there is freedom (2 Corinthians 3:17).
- I am dead to sin and alive to God in Christ Jesus (Romans 6:11).
- I walk in the glorious liberty of the children of God (Romans 8:21).

Prayer (From Day 19: Freedom in Christ)

Father God, thank You for the freedom I have in Christ. Help me to walk daily in that freedom and not return to old habits, fears, or mindsets. Remind me that I am redeemed, forgiven, and restored. Teach me to live boldly and joyfully in the liberty You have given me. In Jesus' name, Amen.

Day 20: Power of the Holy Spirit
Inspirational Quote

"The Holy Spirit does not make you stronger for yourself alone—He empowers you to live boldly for God's glory."

Scriptures

- "But you will receive power when the Holy Spirit comes on you; and you will be My witnesses..." (Acts 1:8)

- "Now to Him who is able to do immeasurably more than all we ask or imagine, according to His power that is at work within us." (Ephesians 3:20)

Declarations

1. I declare that I am empowered by the Holy Spirit.
2. The power of God is actively working within me.
3. I declare that the Holy Spirit strengthens me for every assignment.
4. I am bold and courageous through the Spirit of God.
5. I declare that God's power enables me to overcome every obstacle.
6. The Holy Spirit equips me to walk in purpose and authority.
7. I live each day guided and strengthened by the power of the Holy Spirit.

Encouraging Affirmations

Speak these truths over yourself daily and walk confidently in the Spirit's power:

- I receive power through the Holy Spirit (Acts 1:8).
- The same power that raised Christ from the dead lives in me (Romans 8:11).
- God's power is made perfect in my weakness (2 Corinthians 12:9).
- I can do all things through Christ who strengthens me (Philippians 4:13).
- The Holy Spirit helps me in my weakness (Romans 8:26).
- I am strengthened with power through His Spirit in my inner being (Ephesians 3:16).
- Greater is He who is in me than he who is in the world (1 John 4:4).

Prayer

Holy Spirit, thank You for filling me with Your power. Strengthen me where I am weak and guide me in every decision I make. Help me to walk boldly, live faithfully, and reflect Christ in all I do. Let Your power flow through my life for Your glory. In Jesus' name, Amen.

Day 21: Spiritual Growth

Inspirational Quote

"Spiritual growth is not about perfection—it is about daily surrender and steady progress in Christ."

Scriptures

- "But grow in the grace and knowledge of our Lord and Savior Jesus Christ." (2 Peter 3:18)
- "Being confident of this, that He who began a good work in you will carry it on to completion until the day of Christ Jesus." (Philippians 1:6)

Declarations

1. I declare that I am continually growing in my relationship with Christ.
2. God is developing my character and strengthening my faith.
3. I declare that His Word transforms my heart and mind daily.
4. I am rooted and built up in Christ.
5. I declare that every season produces spiritual maturity in me.
6. The Holy Spirit shapes me into the image of Jesus.

7. I am becoming stronger, wiser, and more grounded in my faith each day.

Encouraging Affirmations

Speak these truths over yourself daily and embrace steady spiritual growth:

- I grow in the grace and knowledge of Jesus Christ (2 Peter 3:18).
- He who began a good work in me will complete it (Philippians 1:6).
- I am rooted and built up in Christ (Colossians 2:7).
- God's Word nourishes and strengthens my spirit (Matthew 4:4).
- The righteous flourish like a palm tree (Psalm 92:12).
- I bear fruit as I remain connected to the Vine (John 15:5).
- The Holy Spirit produces fruit in my life (Galatians 5:22–23).

Prayer

Father God, thank You for working in my life every day. Help me to grow in grace, wisdom, and spiritual maturity. Teach me through every season and shape me into the person You have called me to be. Strengthen my faith and deepen my relationship with You. In Jesus' name, Amen.

Day 22: Walking in Humility
Inspirational Quote

"True humility is not thinking less of yourself—it is thinking of yourself less and Christ more."

Scriptures

- "Humble yourselves before the Lord, and He will lift you up." (James 4:10)
- "Do nothing out of selfish ambition or vain conceit. Rather, in humility value others above yourselves." (Philippians 2:3)

Declarations

1. I declare that I walk in humility before God and others.
2. I choose to serve rather than seek recognition.
3. I declare that pride has no place in my heart.
4. I value others and treat them with kindness and respect.
5. I humble myself before the Lord, trusting Him to lift me up.

6. I follow Christ's example of obedience and
    servanthood.

7. My strength comes from surrendering to God's will.

Encouraging Affirmations

Speak these truths over yourself daily and cultivate
a humble heart:

- God gives grace to the humble (James 4:6).

- I clothe myself with humility toward others (1 Peter
  5:5).

- The Lord guides the humble in what is right (Psalm
  25:9).

- I follow the example of Christ, who humbled
  Himself (Philippians 2:8).

- I serve the Lord with a gentle and quiet spirit (1
  Peter 3:4).

- Humility leads to honor and life (Proverbs 22:4).

- I decrease so that Christ may increase in my life
  (John 3:30).

Prayer

Father God, teach me to walk in humility each day.
Guard my heart from pride and selfish ambition.
Help me to reflect the servant heart of Jesus in my

words and actions. May my life bring You honor and glory. In Jesus' name, Amen.

Day 23: Walking in Forgiveness

Inspirational Quote

"Forgiveness is not a sign of weakness—it is a reflection of God's strength working in you."

Scriptures

- "Be kind and compassionate to one another, forgiving each other, just as in Christ God forgave you." (Ephesians 4:32)
- "If we confess our sins, He is faithful and just and will forgive us our sins and purify us from all unrighteousness." (1 John 1:9)

Declarations

1. I declare that I am forgiven and redeemed through Christ.
2. I release every offense and choose to forgive freely.
3. I declare that bitterness has no place in my heart.
4. I forgive others as God has forgiven me.

5. I walk in peace because I have surrendered every hurt to God.

6. I declare that God heals my heart and restores my joy.

7. I choose grace over resentment and freedom over offense.

Encouraging Affirmations

Speak these truths over yourself daily and walk in the freedom of forgiveness:

- I have been forgiven and cleansed by the blood of Jesus (1 John 1:9).

- As far as the east is from the west, so far has God removed my transgressions (Psalm 103:12).

- There is now no condemnation for those who are in Christ Jesus (Romans 8:1).

- I forgive as the Lord forgave me (Colossians 3:13).

- God heals the brokenhearted and binds up their wounds (Psalm 147:3).

- I let go of anger and choose love (Ephesians 4:31–32).

- Blessed are the merciful, for they will be shown mercy (Matthew 5:7).

Prayer

Father God, thank You for forgiving me completely and unconditionally. Help me to extend that same grace to others. Heal any hurt in my heart and remove any bitterness or resentment. Teach me to walk daily in forgiveness and freedom. In Jesus' name, Amen.

Day 24: Gratitude and Thanksgiving

Inspirational Quote

"Gratitude turns what we have into enough and invites God's peace into our hearts."

Scriptures

- "Give thanks in all circumstances; for this is God's will for you in Christ Jesus." (1 Thessalonians 5:18)
- "Enter His gates with thanksgiving and His courts with praise; give thanks to Him and praise His name." (Psalm 100:4)

Declarations

1. I declare that I have a grateful heart in every season.
2. I choose thanksgiving over complaint.
3. I declare that God's goodness surrounds my life daily.

4. I give thanks in all circumstances, trusting God's purpose.

5. I declare that gratitude fills my heart with peace and joy.

6. I recognize every good gift as coming from God.

7. My life is an offering of praise and thanksgiving to the Lord.

Encouraging Affirmations

Speak these truths over yourself daily and cultivate a lifestyle of gratitude:

- I give thanks in all circumstances (1 Thessalonians 5:18).
- Every good and perfect gift comes from God (James 1:17).
- I will bless the Lord at all times; His praise will continually be in my mouth (Psalm 34:1).
- The peace of God rules in my heart as I remain thankful (Colossians 3:15).
- I rejoice always and pray continually with thanksgiving (Philippians 4:4–6).
- God's steadfast love endures forever (Psalm 136:1).
- My heart overflows with gratitude for His faithfulness.

Prayer

Father God, thank You for Your countless blessings in my life. Teach me to live with a heart full of gratitude, no matter my circumstances. Help me to focus on Your goodness and faithfulness each day. May my life reflect thanksgiving, praise, and joy. In Jesus' name, Amen.

Day 25: Overcoming the Enemy

Inspirational Quote

"Victory is not achieved by your strength alone, but by standing firm in the power of God."

Scriptures

- "Submit yourselves, then, to God. Resist the devil, and he will flee from you." (James 4:7)
- "The Lord is my light and my salvation—whom shall I fear?" (Psalm 27:1)

Declarations

1. I declare that I have victory through Jesus Christ.
2. I resist every scheme of the enemy in the name of Jesus.

3. I declare that no weapon formed against me shall prosper.

4. I stand firm in the armor of God.

5. The enemy has no authority over my life.

6. I overcome by the blood of the Lamb and the word of my testimony.

7. I walk boldly in the victory God has already secured for me.

Encouraging Affirmations

Speak these truths over yourself daily and stand firm in spiritual victory:

- I submit to God and resist the devil, and he flees from me (James 4:7).
- No weapon formed against me shall prosper (Isaiah 54:17).
- I am more than a conqueror through Christ who loves me (Romans 8:37).
- The Lord is my light and my salvation; I will not fear (Psalm 27:1).
- I put on the full armor of God (Ephesians 6:11).
- Greater is He who is in me than he who is in the world (1 John 4:4).
- Thanks be to God, who gives me the victory through our Lord Jesus Christ (1 Corinthians 15:57).

Prayer

Father God, thank You for the victory I have through Jesus Christ. Help me to stand firm against every attack of the enemy. Clothe me in Your armor and strengthen my faith. Remind me daily that the battle belongs to You and that I walk in victory. In Jesus' name, Amen.

Day 26: God's Love and Compassion

Inspirational Quote

"God's love is constant, His compassion is endless, and His mercy meets you fresh every morning."

Scriptures

- "The Lord is compassionate and gracious, slow to anger, abounding in love." (Psalm 103:8)
- "Because of the Lord's great love we are not consumed, for His compassions never fail." (Lamentations 3:22)

Declarations

1. I declare that I am deeply loved by God.
2. God's compassion toward me is new every morning.

3. I declare that nothing can separate me from the love of Christ.

4. I receive God's mercy and extend compassion to others.

5. I am secure in the unfailing love of my Heavenly Father.

6. I declare that God's love heals and restores my heart.

7. I reflect God's love and compassion in my words and actions.

Encouraging Affirmations

Speak these truths over yourself daily and rest in God's faithful love:

- The Lord is compassionate and gracious toward me (Psalm 103:8).
- His compassions never fail; they are new every morning (Lamentations 3:22–23).
- Nothing can separate me from the love of God in Christ Jesus (Romans 8:38–39).
- God has loved me with an everlasting love (Jeremiah 31:3).
- As a father has compassion on his children, so the Lord has compassion on me (Psalm 103:13).
- I love because He first loved me (1 John 4:19).

- The Lord is good to all and has compassion on all He has made (Psalm 145:9).

Prayer (From Day 26: God's Love and Compassion)

Father God, thank You for Your unfailing love and endless compassion. Help me to fully receive Your mercy and reflect that same love toward others. Heal every broken place in my heart and remind me daily that I am secure in You. May my life be a reflection of Your kindness and grace. In Jesus' name, Amen.

Day 27: Restoring Relationships

Inspirational Quote

"God specializes in restoration—He heals hearts, rebuilds trust, and renews broken relationships."

Scriptures

- "Make every effort to live in peace with everyone." (Hebrews 12:14)
- "Be kind and compassionate to one another, forgiving each other, just as in Christ God forgave you." (Ephesians 4:32)

Declarations

1. I declare that God is restoring broken relationships in my life.
2. I choose forgiveness and release every offense.
3. I declare that peace and reconciliation flow into my relationships.
4. My words bring healing and understanding.
5. I humble myself and seek unity where there has been division.
6. God softens hearts and rebuilds trust.
7. I walk in love, grace, and wisdom in every relationship.

Encouraging Affirmations

Speak these truths over yourself daily and believe for restoration:

- I pursue peace with everyone (Hebrews 12:14).
- I forgive as the Lord forgave me (Colossians 3:13).
- A gentle answer turns away wrath (Proverbs 15:1).
- God heals the brokenhearted and binds up their wounds (Psalm 147:3).
- I am a peacemaker and reflect God's love (Matthew 5:9).
- Love covers a multitude of sins (1 Peter 4:8).

- The Lord restores what has been broken (Joel 2:25).

Prayer
Father God, thank You for being a God of restoration. Heal any brokenness in my relationships and give me the humility to seek peace. Teach me to forgive quickly and love deeply. Restore trust, renew unity, and let Your grace flow in every connection. In Jesus' name, Amen.

Day 28: Renewing Your Mind
Inspirational Quote
"When you renew your mind with God's truth, you transform the direction of your life."

Scriptures
- "Do not conform to the pattern of this world, but be transformed by the renewing of your mind." (Romans 12:2)
- "Set your minds on things above, not on earthly things." (Colossians 3:2)

Declarations

1. I declare that my mind is being renewed by God's Word.
2. I reject negative and destructive thoughts.
3. I declare that my thoughts are aligned with God's truth.
4. I take every thought captive and make it obedient to Christ.
5. My mind is focused on what is pure, true, and praiseworthy.
6. I am transformed daily by the power of God's Word.
7. I have the mind of Christ.

Encouraging Affirmations

Speak these truths over yourself daily and allow God to shape your thinking:

- I am transformed by the renewing of my mind (Romans 12:2).
- I set my mind on things above (Colossians 3:2).
- I take every thought captive to obey Christ (2 Corinthians 10:5).

- I think on whatever is true, noble, right, pure, and lovely (Philippians 4:8).
- I have the mind of Christ (1 Corinthians 2:16).
- God's Word is a lamp to my feet and a light to my path (Psalm 119:105).
- The peace of God guards my heart and mind in Christ Jesus (Philippians 4:7).

Prayer

Father God, renew my mind daily through Your Word. Help me to reject lies and embrace truth. Transform my thoughts so they align with Your will and purpose for my life. Guard my mind with Your peace and guide my thinking in righteousness. In Jesus' name, Amen.

Day 29: Breaking Strongholds

Inspirational Quote

"Strongholds fall when God's truth rises."

Scriptures

- "For the weapons of our warfare are not carnal, but mighty through God to the pulling down of strongholds." (2 Corinthians 10:4)
- "You will know the truth, and the truth will set you free." (John 8:32)

Declarations

1. I declare that every stronghold in my life is broken in the name of Jesus.
2. I pull down lies and replace them with God's truth.
3. I declare that I am free from fear, addiction, doubt, and negative thinking.
4. The power of God demolishes every spiritual barrier.
5. I take every thought captive and make it obedient to Christ.
6. I declare that chains are broken and freedom is mine.
7. I walk in the authority given to me through Jesus Christ.

Encouraging Affirmations

Speak these truths over yourself daily and stand firm in spiritual victory:

- The weapons of my warfare are mighty through God (2 Corinthians 10:4).
- The truth of God sets me free (John 8:32).
- No weapon formed against me shall prosper (Isaiah 54:17).
- I overcome by the blood of the Lamb and the word of my testimony (Revelation 12:11).
- Greater is He who is in me than he who is in the world (1 John 4:4).
- I have authority to overcome all the power of the enemy (Luke 10:19).
- Where the Spirit of the Lord is, there is freedom (2 Corinthians 3:17).

Prayer

Father God, I thank You for the authority and freedom I have in Christ. Break every stronghold in my mind, heart, and life that is not from You. Replace every lie with Your truth. Strengthen me to stand firm and walk in the freedom You have given me. In Jesus' name, Amen.

Day 30: Abiding in Christ

Inspirational Quote

"When you remain in Christ, your strength is sustained, your faith is steady, and your life bears fruit."

Scriptures

- "Abide in Me, and I in you…" (John 15:4)
- "I am the vine; you are the branches…" (John 15:5)

Declarations

1. I declare that I remain connected to Christ, my true Vine.
2. My strength and life flow from my relationship with Jesus.
3. I declare that I bear lasting spiritual fruit.
4. I depend on Christ in every area of my life.
5. I stay rooted and grounded in His Word.
6. I declare that my faith grows stronger as I abide in Him.
7. My life reflects Christ because I remain close to Him.

Encouraging Affirmations

Speak these truths over yourself daily and stay rooted in Christ:

- I abide in Christ, and He abides in me (John 15:4).

- Apart from Him, I can do nothing (John 15:5).

- I am rooted and built up in Christ (Colossians 2:7).

- God's Word lives and remains in me (John 15:7).

- I bear fruit in every good work (Colossians 1:10).

- The Lord is my portion; I remain secure in Him (Psalm 16:5).

- I flourish like a tree planted by streams of water (Psalm 1:2–3).

Prayer

Father God, help me to abide in Christ daily. Keep my heart connected to You and my mind focused on Your truth. Teach me to depend on You completely and to bear fruit that glorifies Your name. Strengthen my faith and draw me closer to You every day. In Jesus' name, Amen.

Day 31: Living a Life of Praise

Inspirational Quote

"Praise is not just a song you sing—it is a lifestyle you live."

Scriptures

- "I will bless the Lord at all times..." (Psalm 34:1)

- "Let us continually offer to God a sacrifice of praise..." (Hebrews 13:15)

Declarations

1. I declare that praise is continually on my lips.
2. I choose worship in every season of life.
3. I declare that my heart is filled with gratitude and thanksgiving.
4. I praise God in both victories and challenges.
5. My life reflects honor and glory to the Lord.
6. I declare that praise shifts my focus from problems to God's power.
7. I live each day as an offering of worship to Him.

Encouraging Affirmations

Speak these truths over yourself daily and cultivate a lifestyle of praise:

- I bless the Lord at all times (Psalm 34:1).
- I offer a continual sacrifice of praise (Hebrews 13:15).
- Let everything that has breath praise the Lord (Psalm 150:6).
- The Lord inhabits the praises of His people (Psalm 22:3).
- I enter His gates with thanksgiving and His courts with praise (Psalm 100:4).

- The joy of the Lord is my strength (Nehemiah 8:10).
- Great is the Lord, and greatly to be praised (Psalm 145:3).

Prayer

Father God, I thank You for who You are and all You have done. Teach me to live a life of continual praise. Let worship flow from my heart in every circumstance. May my words, actions, and thoughts glorify You daily. Fill me with joy as I honor You with my life. In Jesus' name, Amen.

Conclusion

Congratulations on completing *31 Days of Declarations: A Journey of Faith, Hope, and Victory*. Over the past month, you have taken intentional steps to declare God's truth over your life, align your heart with His promises, and strengthen your faith.

Each declaration has been a seed planted in your spirit. As you continue to water these seeds with prayer, meditation, and faith, you will begin to see them bear fruit in your life.

This journey does not end here. The truths you have spoken and the promises you have embraced

are tools you can carry into every season.
Whenever doubt, fear, or discouragement arises,
return to these declarations and boldly proclaim
God's Word. His promises are timeless, and His
faithfulness endures forever.

Transformation is a process. As Romans 12:2
reminds us, you are renewed as your mind is
transformed. Every declaration brings you closer to
the abundant life God has prepared for you.

As You Move Forward

- Keep speaking life. Your words carry power.
- Trust the process. God is working even when you
  cannot see it.
- Stay rooted in His Word. Let it remain your
  foundation.
- Share what you have learned. Be a light to others.
  As you continue this journey of faith, know that
  God is with you every step of the way. You are
  loved, chosen, and called for a purpose.

The journey does not end here—it is only the
beginning. Keep declaring, keep believing, and
watch God move mightily in your life.

In His Love and Grace,

Dr. Tyrone Lewis, Sr.

Confession on Forgiveness

I declare that I have a heart of forgiveness, and I walk in love and freedom.

I confess that I forgive others as God has forgiven me. I release all bitterness, anger, and resentment, and I choose to walk in peace and grace. I let go of every hurt and offense, knowing that forgiveness brings healing and restoration to my soul (Ephesians 4:31–32).

I decree that I am free from the chains of unforgiveness. I will not allow grudges or offenses to take root in my heart. I choose to forgive quickly and completely, just as Christ has forgiven me (Colossians 3:13).

I declare that I release those who have hurt or wronged me. I bless them and pray for them, trusting God to bring justice and healing in every situation. I refuse to allow unforgiveness to hinder my prayers or my relationship with God (Mark 11:25).

I confess that forgiveness does not make me weak, but strengthens me. It frees me from the past and opens the door for God's blessings to flow in my life. I choose to walk in love and extend grace, even when it is difficult, because Christ's love empowers me to forgive.

I decree that I am no longer controlled by pain or offense. I am healed, whole, and at peace. My heart is guarded by God's love, and I am free from the weight of bitterness and unforgiveness (Matthew 6:14–15).

I declare that I forgive myself for past mistakes and failures. I choose to see myself as God sees me— redeemed, loved, and worthy of grace. I let go of shame and guilt, and I walk in the fullness of God's forgiveness and mercy.

In Jesus' name, I live a life of forgiveness, walking in freedom, love, and peace. Amen.

Confession on Health

I declare that my body is the temple of the Holy Spirit, redeemed, cleansed, and sanctified by the blood of Jesus.

I decree that every organ, tissue, and cell in my body functions in divine order, just as God designed it. Sickness, disease, and pain have no authority in my life because I am healed by the stripes of Jesus (Isaiah 53:5).I speak life and strength to my immune system, energy to my body, and clarity to my mind. I declare that I walk in divine health, free from fear and anxiety about my well-being. The same

Spirit that raised Christ from the dead dwells in me, giving life to my mortal body (Romans 8:11).

I reject and cancel every word, thought, or diagnosis that does not align with the Word of God. I declare that healing is my inheritance, and I receive it by faith. No weapon formed against my health shall prosper (Isaiah 54:17), and I will live to declare the works of the Lord (Psalm 118:17).

I speak over my life that I will flourish in health, vitality, and strength, fulfilling every purpose God has for me. I trust in the Lord as my healer and Great Physician. His Word is life to me and health to all my flesh (Proverbs 4:20–22).

In Jesus' name, I am strong, whole, and healed. Amen.

Confession on Finances

I declare that I am blessed and highly favored by God.

I decree that I walk in financial abundance, and all my needs are met according to God's riches in glory through Christ Jesus (Philippians 4:19). I am not bound by lack, poverty, or debt, but I am a child of the King, and I have access to His unlimited resources.

I speak increase, overflow, and supernatural provision into my finances. I declare that I am a wise steward of everything God has entrusted to me. I honor the Lord with my wealth, and as I sow generously, I reap generously (2 Corinthians 9:6).

I decree that doors of opportunity, promotion, and favor are opening for me. I am the head and not the tail, above and not beneath (Deuteronomy 28:13). I walk in wisdom and make sound financial decisions. My hands are blessed, and everything I put my hands to prospers (Deuteronomy 28:12).

I reject fear, worry, and anxiety over money because God is my source and my provider. The Lord gives me the power to create wealth and establishes His covenant with me (Deuteronomy 8:18).

I declare that I am a lender and not a borrower (Deuteronomy 28:12). I give cheerfully, and it is given back to me—pressed down, shaken together, and running over (Luke 6:38). Blessings are chasing me down, and I have more than enough to meet my needs and bless others. In Jesus' name, I am financially free, walking in abundance, and living in God's overflow. Amen.

Confession on Discernment

I declare that I have the mind of Christ and walk in wisdom and understanding.

I confess that I am guided by the Holy Spirit in every decision I make. I have clarity of thought and spiritual insight to distinguish between right and wrong, truth and deception. I reject confusion, fear, and doubt, and I walk in discernment that comes from God.

I decree that my heart is sensitive to the leading of the Spirit, and I hear God's voice clearly. I am not swayed by emotions, circumstances, or the opinions of others, but I am rooted in truth. I test all things and hold fast to what is good (1 Thessalonians 5:21).

I declare that I walk in wisdom and make sound decisions that align with God's will for my life. My discernment is sharp, and I see beyond appearances to deeper truths. I avoid distractions and stay focused on my God-given purpose.

I confess that I am not deceived by the enemy's schemes or the world's lies. I recognize what is from God and reject anything that does not align with His Word. I have spiritual eyes to see and ears to hear, and I am led by peace in every situation.

I decree that my discernment grows stronger every day. I am equipped to navigate life with wisdom, understanding, and confidence. I trust God to guide my steps and give me insight into every decision and opportunity.

I declare that I live a life of integrity and purpose, making choices that honor God and bless others. I walk in the light of discernment, and I am a vessel for God's wisdom and truth in the world.

In Jesus' name, I have divine discernment, and I walk in clarity, wisdom, and truth. Amen.

Confession on the Mind

I declare that I have the mind of Christ, and my thoughts are aligned with God's Word.

I decree that my mind is clear, focused, and filled with peace. I reject every thought of fear, doubt, confusion, or negativity, and I take every thought captive to the obedience of Christ (2 Corinthians 10:5). My mind is a place of faith, hope, and positivity, and I refuse to allow the enemy to infiltrate it with lies.

I declare that God's peace guards my heart and mind in Christ Jesus (Philippians 4:7). I think on things that are true, noble, right, pure, lovely, and praiseworthy

(Philippians 4:8). My thoughts are filled with God's truth, and His Word renews and transforms my mind daily (Romans 12:2).

I decree that I am not conformed to the patterns of this world, but I am transformed by the renewing of my mind. I have divine wisdom, understanding, and clarity in every decision I make. God gives me insight and revelation to navigate every situation with confidence and purpose.

I reject the spirit of fear, for God has not given me a spirit of fear, but of power, love, and a sound mind (2 Timothy 1:7). My mind is disciplined, and I am focused on God's promises, not my problems.

I declare that no weapon formed against my mind shall prosper (Isaiah 54:17). I dwell in perfect peace because my mind is stayed on the Lord (Isaiah 26:3). I have victory in my thoughts, and I walk in complete mental freedom through the power of Christ.

In Jesus' name, my mind is strong, sound, and filled with God's truth. Amen.

Confession on Supernatural Blessings

I declare that I am walking in the supernatural blessings of God!

I decree that God's favor surrounds me like a shield (Psalm 5:12), and His blessings are overtaking me in every area of my life (Deuteronomy 28:2). I am positioned under an open heaven, and I receive divine provision, promotion, and increase that only God can give.

I declare that I am blessed in the city and blessed in the field, blessed going out and blessed coming in (Deuteronomy 28:3–6). Everything I touch is blessed, and my storehouses overflow with abundance. I am not limited by natural circumstances because I serve a supernatural God who supplies all my needs according to His riches in glory (Philippians 4:19).

I decree that supernatural doors of opportunity are opening for me. God's favor is creating pathways for blessings, and His hand is moving on my behalf. I have divine connections, unexpected resources, and miraculous breakthroughs in my finances, relationships, and endeavors.

I declare that I am highly favored by God and man (Luke 2:52). I walk in supernatural wisdom, discernment, and divine strategy. I do not strive or toil, but rest in the supernatural grace of God that works all things together for my good (Romans 8:28).

I reject every spirit of lack, limitation, and delay, and I decree that the windows of heaven are open over my life. Blessings are being poured out that I do not have room enough to contain (Malachi 3:10). I walk in the overflow, and I am a blessing to others because of the abundance God has entrusted to me.

In Jesus' name, I declare that supernatural blessings are chasing me down, overtaking me, and manifesting in every area of my life. Amen.

Confession on Family

I declare that my family is blessed, protected, and walking in the purpose and promises of God.

I decree that my household serves the Lord with unity, love, and faithfulness (Joshua 24:15). Peace reigns in my home, and the love of God binds us together in perfect harmony (Colossians 3:14). Every relationship in my family is strengthened, restored, and filled with God's presence.

I declare that my family walks in divine health, prosperity, and favor. No weapon formed against us shall prosper, and every plan of the enemy against my family is canceled in Jesus' name (Isaiah 54:17). We are covered by the blood of Jesus, and we dwell in the secret place of the Most High, under His protection and care (Psalm 91:1).

I decree that my children are taught of the Lord, and great is their peace (Isaiah 54:13). They are strong, healthy, wise, and walk in the fear of the Lord. They are leaders in their generation, fulfilling God's purpose for their lives with boldness and confidence.

I speak unity over my marriage and declare that it is built on the foundation of God's Word. Love, respect, and understanding flow freely between us, and we honor God in our relationship. Our marriage is a testimony of His goodness and grace.

I declare that my family is a household of faith. We walk in obedience to God's Word, and we trust Him to guide, provide, and sustain us in every season. We are blessed coming in and blessed going out (Deuteronomy 28:6).

I decree that generational blessings flow through my family. We break every curse, cycle, and stronghold from the past, and we walk in freedom, joy, and victory. God's promises are established in my family for generations to come.

In Jesus' name, my family is a beacon of light, love, and hope in this world. We are blessed, protected, and prospering in every way. Amen.

Confession on Protection

I declare that I am divinely protected by the Lord, and no harm shall come near me or my family.

I decree that the Lord is my refuge and fortress, my God in whom I trust (Psalm 91:2). He covers me with His feathers, and under His wings I find safety (Psalm 91:4). His faithfulness is my shield and defense.

I declare that no weapon formed against me shall prosper, and every tongue that rises against me in judgment will be condemned (Isaiah 54:17). The plans of the enemy are nullified and powerless in my life. I walk in victory, knowing that the Lord fights for me.

I decree that angels are encamped around me and my loved ones, guarding us in all our ways (Psalm 34:7). They lift us up and protect us from danger, harm, and destruction (Psalm 91:11–12).

I declare that I dwell in the secret place of the Most High and abide under the shadow of the Almighty (Psalm 91:1). The Lord is my protector, and His presence surrounds me as a shield (Psalm 5:12). No evil shall befall me, and no plague shall come near my dwelling (Psalm 91:10).

I decree that the blood of Jesus covers me, my home, and my family. Every door and window of my life is sealed with

His protection. The enemy has no access or authority over me because I am hidden in Christ.

I declare that I will not fear the terror of the night, nor the arrows that fly by day, nor the pestilence that stalks in darkness (Psalm 91:5–6). The Lord is my strength and my defense; He is my salvation.

In Jesus' name, I am safe, secure, and divinely protected. The Lord watches over me, and His hand is upon me. Amen.

Confession on Spiritual Warfare

I declare that I am strong in the Lord and in the power of His might.

I put on the full armor of God and stand firm against every scheme of the enemy (Ephesians 6:10–11). I am not afraid, for greater is He who is in me than he who is in the world (1 John 4:4). No weapon formed against me shall prosper, and every tongue that rises against me in judgment I condemn (Isaiah 54:17).

I take authority over every lie, attack, and scheme of the enemy. I declare that I am victorious because I have been given power to tread on serpents, scorpions, and over all the power of the enemy, and nothing shall by any means harm me (Luke 10:19).

I confess that I walk by faith and not by sight. I quench every fiery dart of the enemy with the shield of faith, and I wield the sword of the Spirit, which is the Word of God (Ephesians 6:16–17). I declare that my prayers are powerful and effective, tearing down strongholds and breaking chains (James 5:16; 2 Corinthians 10:4).

I decree that I am covered by the blood of Jesus. The enemy has no hold over me, my family, or my purpose. I reject fear, doubt, and intimidation, and I stand firm in my identity as a child of God. I resist the devil, and he must flee from me (James 4:7).

I declare that I am surrounded by God's protection. Angels are encamped around me, guarding me in all my ways (Psalm 91:11). I walk in victory because Christ has already defeated the enemy. I am more than a conqueror through Him who loved me (Romans 8:37).

I confess that I walk in boldness, strength, and authority. I overcome every obstacle and defeat every attack because the battle is the Lord's, and He fights for me. I will not grow weary, for I know that my God is mighty, and His plans for me will prevail.

In Jesus' name, I declare that I am victorious, unshaken, and walking in divine power and authority. Amen.

Confession on Breaking Strongholds

I declare that every stronghold in my life is broken by the power of God.

I confess that the weapons of my warfare are not carnal but mighty through God for pulling down strongholds (2 Corinthians 10:4). I take authority over every thought, habit, or mindset that exalts itself against the knowledge of God, and I bring every thought captive to the obedience of Christ (2 Corinthians 10:5).

I decree that I am no longer bound by fear, doubt, addiction, or sin. The power of the enemy is broken in my life, and I walk in freedom through Christ Jesus. Strongholds of the past no longer have a hold on me, for I have been set free by the truth of God's Word (John 8:32).

I declare that I am transformed by the renewing of my mind (Romans 12:2). Every lie, false belief, and negative pattern is replaced by the truth of God's promises. I think on things that are true, noble, pure, lovely, and praiseworthy (Philippians 4:8).

I confess that I am no longer defined by my past mistakes, failures, or struggles. I am a new creation in Christ, and old things have passed away (2 Corinthians 5:17). Strongholds of shame, guilt, and condemnation have been destroyed, and I walk in the victory of God's grace and mercy.

I decree that the Spirit of God empowers me to overcome every stronghold. I walk in the Spirit and do not fulfill the desires of the flesh (Galatians 5:16). The power of Christ in me is greater than any power of the enemy (1 John 4:4).

I declare that every generational stronghold, curse, or pattern is broken in Jesus' name. I am covered by the blood of Jesus, and my family and future generations are free from bondage. The blessings of God flow in my life, and I walk in His freedom and favor.

In Jesus' name, I am free from every stronghold, walking in victory, and living in the power of God's truth. Amen.

Confession on Overcoming Lust

I declare that I am free from the power of lust and walk in purity and self-control.

I confess that my body is a temple of the Holy Spirit, and I honor God with my thoughts, words, and actions (1

Corinthians 6:19–20). I reject every thought, desire, or temptation that does not align with God's will for my life. I have been set free from the bondage of sin, and I walk in victory through Christ Jesus.

I decree that my mind is renewed daily by the Word of God (Romans 12:2). I fix my thoughts on things that are true, noble, right, pure, lovely, and praiseworthy (Philippians 4:8). I take every thought captive and make it obedient to Christ (2 Corinthians 10:5).

I declare that I am led by the Spirit and not by the desires of the flesh (Galatians 5:16). The fruit of the Spirit—self-control, love, and purity—flows in and through me. I reject lust and every form of impurity, and I choose to walk in holiness and righteousness.

I confess that I am strengthened by God's grace to overcome every temptation (1 Corinthians 10:13). I do not give in to the desires of my flesh, for I am empowered by the Holy Spirit to rise above them. My strength comes from the Lord, and I am victorious over every struggle.

I decree that my eyes, ears, and heart are guarded by God's truth. I will not set anything impure before my eyes (Psalm 101:3), and I will not entertain thoughts or actions that dishonor God. I walk in the light and reject the darkness of lust and temptation.

I declare that I am a new creation in Christ (2 Corinthians 5:17). My past no longer defines me, and I am free from guilt, shame, and condemnation. I am clothed in the righteousness of Christ, and I choose to live a life that reflects His character.

In Jesus' name, I am free from lust, walking in purity, and living in the power of God's Spirit. Amen.

NOTES